Agile Project Management

Scrum for Beginners

Markus Heimrath

Contents

Glossary

Agile: an approach to software development that is product-orientated, bringing independent teams together and moving forward incrementally.

Agile Development: developing software using the principles of agile project management.

Artefact: the product backlog, sprint backlog and product increments

Burndown chart: A visual representation of project progress.

Conditions of Satisfaction: Conditions for a filing in the product backlog

Daily Scrum: daily scrum team meeting

Definition of Done: definition of the conditions an item or increment has to meet to be considered done

Definition of Ready conditions for a product in sprint to be considered done.

Development Team everyone involved in programming, testing and design

Feature: a function which must be present in the software

Framework: an approach to developing software. Scrum is one example of an Agile framework

Gantt-Chart: representation of project progress in the waterfall model

Increment: a version of a product developed in a sprint

Item: an element of the software under development which is set down in the product backlog

Lean Manufacturing: a modern approach which eliminates waste and is characterised by having few hierarchical structures

Product Backlog: a list of all the desired functions and descriptions of a product

Product Owner: the team member responsible for looking after the product, leading the team and managing costs

Requirements: functions stipulated by the customer, usually associated with waterfall projects

Roles: Scrum includes several roles which have clearly defined responsibilities and places in the organisational structure. Two key examples are the Product Owner and the Scrum Master

Scrum: a term taken from the sport of rugby, now used for an approach to software development

Scrum Manifesto: the first written definition of the principles of scrum

Scrum Master: the Scrum Master facilitates the organisational aspects of the team, but not the content of their work; they are responsible for the process

Sprint: a period of time - generally 2-4 weeks - in which specific tasks must be completed

Sprint Backlog: a list of all the tasks targeted to be delivered during a sprint

Sprint Retrospective: reviewing the process of a completed sprint

Sprint Review: reviewing the outcomes of a sprint

Stakeholders: everyone involved in a project who are not part of the scrum team itself

Story Points: units of measurement on the burndown chart

Timeboxed: allocating a specific period of time for a task or meeting

User Story: a description of the product from the user's perspective

Waterfall Methodology: traditional project management whose structure resembles a waterfall. It proceeds from beginning to end according to a project plan with reference to milestones.

1. Introduction

If you come up with an idea for a product nowadays you can bring it to market within a month. All you need is modern software as your design tools, digital nomads as your workforce and a globally integrated logistics system. But increasing the speed of production means changing how we work. The first to recognise this were Japanese car manufacturers. But they realised something else, as well: not spotting a mistake until the end of the process causes massive delays to production. It is also incredibly wasteful in terms of time and resources. By adopting lean manufacturing, Toyota sought to make production as smooth and frictionless as flowing water. They did this by constantly checking parts during production so that if a flaw was found, it could be dealt with immediately, even if that meant the production line had to be stopped momentarily.

This new approach, which turns away from centralised and unalterable planning towards dynamic, flexible systems, is central to Agile development. Scrum is part of the Agile movement, which offers an answer to rigid project management. It is the complete opposite of the waterfall approach. Under the waterfall system a project is divided up into phases which build upon each other and are mutually dependent. Specific milestones are set up which have to be reached, along with equally clear goals for each project phase.

The name derives from the cascades which make up a project plan, flowing down from the starting point.

You have probably worked on a project like this yourself. It remains the most widespread approach - probably because everyone's always done it that way. Businesses, and large organisations in particular, hate change of any kind, so they stick with the tried-and-tested Excel spreadsheets, PowerPoint presentations and waterfall projects.

This book will show you how Agile and Scrum are superior to the waterfall approach in many key areas. They save costs, drive quality and reduce unnecessary administrative processes (though that's not to say there's no administration required at all). If you've always been one of those project managers who drove their team forward from one milestone to the next, never losing sight of the project plan, then Scrum gives you the chance to relax a little, because the focus is all on teamwork.

One key idea behind Agile is letting people who know what they're doing get on with their work . You won't find a business developer who knows nothing about coding spending months defining the requirements for a new app. It's about teams working together from the very start, collaborating, creating the greatest possible degree of transparency and goal orientation.

The waterfall method always conceals the danger that the project plan is king. What matters in Scrum is the product itself. And let's get another preconception out of the way while we're at it: Scrum isn't just a student debating society, and just because any member of the team can contribute doesn't mean that everything turns into a talking shop. There are meetings, but generally they end up being shorter than their equivalents in waterfall projects. What matters most is a shared vision of the project: after all, many eyes see more than two. That also means the that members of the development team should be ready to help each other, even if it isn't specifically their job. The goal is to complete the sprint and deliver "potentially shippable products."

2. Scrum/Waterfall Hybrids

It's a fact of life that any given system, process or framework generate a certain level of discussion about doctrinal purity. The roles and processes in Scrum are clearly defined and their number is easily managed. Nonetheless, many Scrum developers treat these rules as articles of faith and will admit of no changes to them. At times, however, reality demands something other than pure theory alone.

An Example:

You're a software developer working for a large organisation. Management expect you to submit monthly reports, but that goes against the rules of Scrum. So you've got a choice: either give up on Scrum and the Agile framework, or accept a compromise and, as the Product Owner, write a monthly report. And, because the report will never be read by your team and it will never influence the project itself, this is a compromise you can accept without any reservation.

Another Example:

You've been asked to develop some in-house software and you've put together a Scrum team. But your divisional manager wants to see and approve all products at the end of each sprint. This is a compromise you shouldn't accept, as it goes against the basic rules of Definition of Done and the team's individual personal responsibility.

As a Scrum expert you may find yourself asked to be part of a waterfall project, and there are ways of making this work. For example, you could treat each cascade as its own Scrum project, aligning the two systems that way. More than the terms we use, what makes Scrum work are the values and attitudes associated with it. As long as the priority is developing the product and its value, and the team can work independently and dynamically, then a hybrid form is by all means possible. You will often find project plans being drawn up, despite what the Scrum framework sets out. Even stakeholders who are familiar with Scrum often expect some such document because they find it easier to understand. As long as it's clear to everyone involved that milestones should not be considered mutually dependent sprints, and that the plan is more of a time allowance than a script, then this, too, shouldn't be a problem.

The Story of the Pig and the Chicken

Once upon a time, a pig and a chicken were sitting under a tree and wondering what the future held for them. Suddenly the hen said, "Hey, I've got an idea. Let's open a restaurant. We'll call it 'Ham and Eggs'." The pig thought for a moment and shook his head. "Thanks, but no thanks. You'll be happy to lay out your contribution and perch in the background but I'll be the one putting my back into it."

In a Scrum Team the developers are the pigs and the stakeholders are the hens. These aren't perhaps the best terms to use every day, but they help represent the relationship. The British software developers Swordfish Studios prefer the terms 'pirates' and 'ninjas'. The pirates are the hens: They board your ship, loot everything they can and sail away, leaving only chaos behind. This is, of course, a rather exaggerated description of the role of the stakeholders. When asked why they chose ninjas as the opposite of pirates, the developers said, "Because ninjas are cool." Needless to say, this story has given rise to a whole genre of internet memes.

3. A Brief History of Scrum

The origins of the term "Scrum" can be traced back to two programmers, Jeff Sutherland and Ken Schwaber, who were the first to use it back in the early '90s. They introduced the term at a conference in Austin, Texas, in 1995 and in the title of their paper, "Scrum Software Development Process".

'Scrum' isn't an acronym which you have to break up into different concepts. It actually comes from the game of rugby. A 'scrum' in rugby is a which may look chaotic to the outsider but in reality it is a closely co-ordinated effort to progress the ball further up the pitch.

Sutherland and Schwaber were inspired by Ikujiro Takeuchi and Hirotaka Nonaka, two Japanese management consultants, who used the term in their 1986 paper, "The New New Product Development Game" as a metaphor for teamwork. This paper was one of the first to show how important teamwork is to product development. The researchers showed an organisation which allows small teams to work independently and sets them goals rather than giving them lists of tasks to complete can achieve the best outcomes in the development of new, complex products. The best teams are the ones who know where they are going, but who are allowed to find their own way to the destination. Nonaka and Takeuchi's key argument was summarised by Gunter Verheyen as "Teams require autonomy to achieve excellence."[1]

These ideas were met with enthusiasm from Sutherland and Schwaber, who saw in them the ideal conditions for software development. They promoted them among other members of the coding community and in February 2001 the Agile Manifesto was published.

The manifesto is short and to-the-point, just as sprint and product backlog entries would later become.

---

[1] Gunther Verheyen, "Scrum - A Pocket Guide, 2nd Ed" VanHarenPublishing; 2nd ed. edition (16 Feb. 2019), p41

3.1 Manifesto for Agile Software Development

"We are uncovering better ways of developing software by doing it and helping others do it."

Through this work we have come to value:

- Individuals and interactions over processes and tools
- Working software over comprehensive documentation
- Customer collaboration over contract negotiation
- Responding to change over following a plan

That is, while there is value in the items on the right, we value the items on the left more.

Many leading developers signed the manifesto in 2001: Kent Beck, Mike Beedle, Arie van Bennekum, Alistair Cockburn, Ward Cunningham, Martin Fowler, James Grenning, Jim Highsmith, Andrew Hunt, Ron Jeffries, Jon Kern, Brian Marick, Robert C. Martin, Steve Mellor, Ken Schwaber, Jeff Sutherland and Dave Thomas.

They also set down **12 Principles** explaining the manifesto in more detail:

1. "Our highest priority is to satisfy the customer through early and continuous delivery of valuable software."

2. "Welcome changing requirements, even late in development. Agile processes harness change for the customer's competitive advantage."

3. "Deliver working software frequently, from a couple of weeks to a couple of months, with a preference to the shorter timescale."

4. "Business people and developers must work together daily throughout the project."

5. "Build projects around motivated individuals. Give them the environment and support they need, and trust them to get the job done."

6. "The most efficient and effective method of conveying information to and within a development team is face-to-face conversation."

7. "Working software is the primary measure of progress."

8. "Agile processes promote sustainable development. The sponsors, developers, and users should be able to maintain a constant pace indefinitely."

9. "Continuous attention to technical excellence and good design enhances agility."

10. "Simplicity--the art of maximizing the amount of work not done--is essential."

11. "The best architectures, requirements, and designs emerge from self-organizing teams."

12. "At regular intervals, the team reflects on how to become more effective, then tunes and adjusts its behavior accordingly."

Agile represents the theoretical framework for software development, while Scrum sets out a concrete, practical introduction to this way of working. In 2001 Schwaber co-authored the first book on the subject: "Agile Software Development with Scrum". Soon afterwards, Sutherland set up his own business providing training seminars and certification in the Scrum framework.

Today Scrum is an important standard in software development. It is the most popular of the various Agile frameworks and has been adopted in other industry sectors.

4. The Principles of Scrum

It's important to get to know the principles of Scrum as they are set down in the Agile Manifesto so you can understand and apply the framework. The next thing you need to know is what Scrum is not: it's not a project based on a detailed plan which you work through step-by-step. There is a plan, but it changes all the time and is less critical than the individual elements which make it up. Traditional projects followed predetermined tasks set down in Gantt-charts, starting at the beginning and working through to the end. Scrum is different. The only thing set down are the goals, and it's left to the teams to find out for themselves the best way to achieve them. Think of working with Scrum like this:

> Imagine you want to ride your mountain bike down a slope. You're standing at the top of the hill and all you can see below you is a forest. To try to draw up a detailed plan at this stage wouldn't just be a waste of time - it could even be dangerous. What you really know is that you want to get to the campsite down there where everyone else is already eating dinner and having a drink. When you set off you can only see the 30-50m ahead of you. Now and then you might stop to check do see if you're heading in generally the right direction, but it's much more important to jump over the tree trunk which has fallen across your path or dodge out of the way of that

deer. It's only because you're constantly adapting your course and how you ride that you make it safely to your goal: a juicy steak and a cold beer.

4.1 Why Scrum?

Before we really wade in it's worth taking a moment to think about what makes Scrum better than other frameworks, especially ones not based on Agile methodology. Scrum's three most important advantages are that it allows rapid adaptation to changing situations, it delivers outstanding results, and it keeps workers satisfied.

Modern software development - like many other products and services - is expected to work at an ever faster pace. There is constant demand for new products, so the business which sets up working parties and 6 months later delivers a 3000-page comprehensive project plan will always be the loser. Markets are always changing, and that's not to mention new software and hardware standards (such as a new version of iOS and Android coming out every year). This means that a project plan is already obsolete the very day it's published. With Scrum the objective is clearly defined (for example: develop a new sat-nav app) but not exactly how that is to be achieved. Questions such as the colour of the UI, the fonts to be used and the registration process are unimportant.

Through constant testing and development, moving forward in little steps, each component of the product is only handed over when it is really "done". This way, a product grows out of different components which have been subject to constant testing and verification. There's no need for final quality testing because this has already taken place during the development process.

Your team will love Scrum because they take complete responsibility and can make the most of their expertise and skills. They aren't limited by targets set by business developers who have no technical knowledge or deadlines which are impossible to meet. Instead they are free to organise themselves and don't have to waste time trying to please the boss who's lurking behind them but hasn't a clue what they're actually doing.

There are **three essential parts** to the **Scrum framework.**

- Artefacts
- Roles
- Sprints

Artefact designates the **Product Backlog**, the **Sprint Backlog** and **Increments**. Simply put, these refer to the product's various features and descriptions, the list of tasks and the respective prototypes. But don't forget that the backlog is never static; it is always changing. Some features will be expanded and others removed, one job may be prioritised and another downgraded, and prototypes will be handed back if they don't meet requirements.

Roles define who is involved in a project and what they have to do. If you own your own business then you are a stakeholder, and your customers are, too. The stakeholders determine what they actually want and how big the budget is. The **Product Owner** is similar to a project manager: they are responsible for the **Product Backlog**, but their main responsibility is keeping an eye on the financial side of the project. The **Scrum Master** on the other hand makes sure the project runs smoothly and that Scrum principles are adhered to. They help solve problems which arise in connection with Scrum. The **Development Team** do the actual work. In Scrum the team is considered a single entity and there are no subordinate roles within it. In practice you will find different roles within a team, such as coders, testers and web designers.

Sprints are the short development cycles where work actually takes place. They include Daily Scrums, Sprint Reviews, Sprint Planning and the Sprint Retrospective. From a time perspective, sprints cover a week or two at most. At the end of a sprint a prototype must be "done". When planning a sprint you must ensure the tasks to be completed are neither too broad or too limited. Every day developers meet briefly with the Scrum Master and Product Owner for the **Daily Scrum**.

4.2 Requirements und User Stories

If you've ever worked on a traditional project you'll know all about the problem of requirements. These are the conditions set down in the project plan as if they were carved in stone. They define the complete feature-set of a given product. A Scrum team knows nothing of requirements such as these. To put it better, the requirements are there, but they change often and are fully interchangeable. This is important: imagine that the requirements state that you have to use a certain API to receive data. But while work is underway it becomes clear that this API is no longer available. In Scrum this isn't a problem: the issue is the data the API delivers, not how it is delivered and where it is stored.

Scrum isn't interested in statistical requirements, but in dynamic user stories. These give a vivid picture of the features which are contained in the product backlog. They are usually set out on cards. When developing software with cards, it might look something like this:

As a user I want my position shown on the map.

The next step is to discuss this. The user story is really a starting point for a discussion about how it can be achieved and which requirements have to be attached to it.

These requirements are generally written out on the back of the card.

Position should be accurate

Position should use GPS data

Position should use Wi-Fi

Position should use mobile data

As the development process goes on these user stories are clarified more and more exactly. At first they serve as a sort of place-holder in the product backlog; later they are replaced by detailed user stories and Requirements.

The level of detail in a user story depends largely on where it will be used or implemented. If it is for a sprint, then it needs to be kept short, but if you need something that illustrates the big picture then it can be more extensive. It's best to start of by thinking of how long each user story will take to implement as a way of measuring their scope. It could be anywhere from a few hours to several months. You'll learn more about the details in the product backlog chapter.

5. Starting a Scrum Project

Now we're ready to start! You've had a great idea or received a request from a customer and you want to make it happen as soon as possible but without skimping on quality. The good news: Scrum will help, so don't worry.

The most important thing about people working together is having a team who get on, understand the goal and, of course, the strategy. If you have someone on your team who has worked with Scrum before, then that's an advantage. Even so, people who've never worked with Scrum can still contribute, though they shouldn't be assigned a role.

5.1 Roles

Scrum uses 'roles' to define the specific areas of responsibility in a project. They must be given to individuals, and cannot be taken on by teams. The holder of each role has no deputy and may not share the role with anyone else. This means that the holders have as much freedom as possible and always function autonomously.

Stakeholders

The exception to this rule is the stakeholders, so let's begin with them. By 'stakeholders' we mean all interested participants in a project. That might be you as the owner of the business or the department head who has been assigned this project by management. It might also include members of other business units such as finance or marketing. When you're writing software for a customer they are also a stakeholder, as are their customers who will eventually use the software. Stakeholders set out the framework of a project and define its goal, but they can also set restrictions at the same time. For example, the software might have to meet certain legal requirements. In this case the regulatory authorities are also stakeholders, even if they never attend meetings. The same applies to the end users. If your customer is going to sell your software to a third party, then they have valid interest, but they cannot be there in person to articulate it.

In large organisations in particular, managers who are involved in the project in specific ways play a special role. They are generally from other business units and represent specific interests. The representative of the accounts department will have an interest in the budget, while the marketing people concern themselves with features. The legal team will want to be sure that there are no breaches of copyright. And ultimately there's also the big cheese at the top (assuming you're not that person) who's paying for the whole shebang.

All these stakeholders can contribute suggestions, set budgets and discuss goals. However, their only contact with the Scrum team is through the Product Owner, whose job it is to integrate the stakeholders' input into the product backlog. No-one else is allowed to contact the stakeholders: not the Scrum Master, not the development team. This is crucial: instructions to the team may **only** come from within the team. A Stakeholder cannot tell a developer what to do. They can't even tell the Product Owner what their priorities should be.

Product Owner

The Product Owner is the interface between the stakeholders and the Developers, but they also need to keep an eye on the budget and the overall marketability of the product. The role is similar to that of a project manager, but they work very differently. A Product Owner needs business acumen and skills, as they are responsible for the financial aspects of the development process at the level of a sprint just as much as at full Release level. Another key responsibility is constructing the product backlog, which forms the foundation of the work of the whole team. That means their technical knowledge is as important as their business acumen. This will come into play in defining the criteria for accepting a release and also monitoring compliance with them. Ultimately they have to work closely with the development team and provide regular feedback to stakeholders.

The Product Owner also has to maintain the product backlog, compiling and refining it as the project progresses, as well as prioritising tasks and estimating timescales. But that doesn't mean you have to do all this on your own. For example, you don't have to draft every single item on the product backlog or estimate how long they will take to develop. Your job is to ensure that estimates are in place and that the priorities allow for constant progression.

You see for yourself that being a Product Owner is a full-time job, not something you can do on the side. It's a job where you have to be able to lead people but also give them as much freedom as possible to take responsibility for the project. The Product Owner must be able to take decisions and take responsibility for them. If you're interested in this role, then it would help a lot if you've already worked on a Scrum project. Project managers with experience of working on traditional projects and additional training in Scrum, perhaps working as a Scrum Master or holding a position of responsibility in a development team are well placed to succeed. If you work for a large organisation you would be particularly well qualified if your department makes a substantial contribution to an internal project. On the other hand, in a project developing products for end-users, it would make more sense if you worked in marketing, product or business development.

It's often the case that stakeholders want to put several Product Owners in place, such as in very extensive projects. This, however, is never a good idea, as in the end it is the Product Owner who has to make the decisions. If you're ever asked if you need an Assistant Product Owner, the answer should always be no. Either you can do the job - in which case you should be left alone to do it - or you can't, and in that case, no assistant or team can help you.

Financial sense must always form the basis for the decisions the Product Owner reaches. So if a project is progressing more slowly than expected, they should focus resources on the most important parts first. If more developers are needed, then careful scrutiny of the budget will determine where money can be saved elsewhere. Saving also means avoiding unnecessary sprint. If a product is completed and tested sooner than planned, then the Product Owner should end the sprint. And if changes in the market, for example, render part of a product no longer worthwhile, they have to be ready to pull the trigger. A case in point would be when a company is working on a LTE chip, but 5G mobile data is introduced sooner than expected.

As the Product Owner you have the most difficult job in the whole Scrum project, but as long as you enjoy taking responsibility and motivating people, it's also the most exciting.

Scrum Master

As Scrum Master you supervise the process and take responsibility for solving problems connected with the process. Your role is similar to that of a trainer, mentor and facilitator. As such, you will need a strong relationship with the development team as well as the Product Owner. You are not responsible for any financial or technical aspects of the process, only for ensuring its smooth operation. Nonetheless, you will need a complete understanding of what the development team is doing. As Scrum Master you serve both the developers and the Product Owner, and it is your task to keep them connected and facilitate effective information sharing. However, if a problem arises it is not your job to tell them what to do, but instead to work with them to develop a solution. As a coach you have no fundamental power to direct other members of the Scrum Team, but if all efforts fail to find an acceptable solution you can use your authority. An example of this would be the development team asking to postpone the Daily Scrum. That goes against the rules and you need to help them understand it is not up for negotiation.

Moreover, you are responsible for preventing disruption. That might be providing each member of the development team with the tools they need, such as a computer with the appropriate software and licences. You will need to ensure their workspace is professional and fit for purpose. That doesn't mean it's your job to refill the coffee machine, but you may need to make sure there is one available to keep your team happy and caffeinated.

The traditional route to becoming a Scrum Master was by working in a development team and taking part in Agile projects. Nowadays, though, you can gain certification through seminars and training. These seminars cover the same material as this book: how the processes work and connect with each other, and how to lead them effectively. Of course, technical knowledge alone won't be enough: you'll need personal and social skills, too. So, while you can keep a cool head and always try to bring people together, as Scrum Master you will also need to be able to stand up for the project and the Scrum philosophy and defend your own position. The good Scrum Master uses their soft skills to lead others, reacts empathetically and understands the complexity of different situations.

The Development Team

The development team is made up of the coders, testers, graphic designers, engineers, network administrators, database managers and UI specialists working on each product iteration. As well as working on the sprint, they should also maintain the product backlog. They will be continuously revising the backlog to keep it up-to-date and negotiating with the Product Owner if changes to priorities are needed or budget issues arise. They also plan sprint and enter them in the sprint backlog. Lastly, they are responsible for testing the product.

The Scrum framework does not break down roles within a team any further than this. However, if you are responsible for putting a team together, your first job is to find the specialists you need. The team should always form a unit. It makes no sense to put all the coders in one group and the UI specialists in another. The collaborative nature of Scrum means they will always work together if a sprint or product requires it. This means there's no need for a specific organisational structure.

The development team should be flexible and highly resilient, as they will not only be working to deadlines on the current sprint backlog but also planning future work.

As well as this, the development team maintains the product backlog. Who is responsible for this at any given time depends on which item in the product backlog is being worked on. It is essential, however, that you ensure this work is done. For example, if a team is working on which functions are shown on a given page within an app, then your UI-specialist will be responsible for the progress on that item. But if it's a question of network structure then the network admins will be the natural point of contact.

The development team has no separate team leader. Their points of contact are the Scrum Master and the Product Owner. The team itself works highly collaboratively and should try to solve problems on its own, organising itself independently according to whatever they're working on.

A development team consists of people who can collaborate and are able to react flexibly, putting the team and the product's success ahead of their own, and who derive satisfaction from creating something together. They need to be top specialists in their fields, but also able to take on other tasks at a moment's notice. If one of your team members likes to remind everyone that 'it's not my job' or 'that's not in my job description', then you should either change their attitude, or, if that isn't possible, get them out of the team.

One of the biggest challenges with a Scrum project is in putting together a team of the right composition and size. If a team is too large it can quickly become uneconomical and negatively impact the budget; too small and the stress of the workload can impact efficiency.

The best way of imagining a team is as a school of fish. There are no alpha-fish in a school who dictate where everyone else is going. And there is no plan that all fish have to follow. Instead, the fish fit in around each other, adapting to different situations. If some fish detect potential prey then they turn towards it and the rest of the school follows. But if others see a predator, they move away from it, changing the course of the whole school. That means each fish is constantly aware of what others are doing, but also keeping its eyes open for prey and predators. The basic rule is this: the first person to see something passes the information on and the school reacts accordingly. It goes without saying that your development team needs to think like this.

5.2 Artefacts: the Product Backlog, Sprint Backlog and Product Increments

Now that we're clear on the roles in a sprint, it's time to consider the tools and the inventory. We've already discussed the product backlog - this plays a central role. You probably know about requirements from previous projects: a comprehensive list which describes all the features of a product under development. The traditional view among project managers was (and to an extent still is), that the more detailed a list is, the better. The problem is that it is very different to make changes further down the line. Hence it's better to think of a product backlog (ideally at least) as a blank slate at first which is gradually filled up as time goes on. The same is broadly true of sprint backlogs, which record the jobs and tasks of classical project management.

A product increment is what has been achieved at the end of a sprint. If all goes according to plan, the finished product is the sum of all the product increments.

5.2.1 The Product Backlog

If you have been given the honour of becoming Product Owner, then the product backlog is one of your most important tools. You are responsible for filling it and making progress through it, as well as ensuring that work is correctly prioritised.

Where do Product Backlogs come from?

A product backlog consists of the product items: basically the features, changes and technical specifications.

An example of a **Feature** might be:

I want a form which sends an e-mail to me.

An example of a **Change** might be:

I want the default sorting order for pictures to be by date and not by name.

A **description of a defect** might be:

Database crashes on upload of images over 2MB.

Lastly, the product backlog list **knowledge-acquisition** work to be undertaken: This might look like this:

Instead of only using VR, we should develop a prototype in 360° and AR and test to determine which is most suitable.

As the Product Owner you don't have to add all product backlog items yourself, but you do have to order them. Try using the DEEP rules:

- Detailed
- Emergent
- Estimated
- Prioritised

Detailed means that items should be described as effectively as possible. Detail is good, but too much detail can cause confusion, while too little detail can leave developers unsure of what they are actually doing. In general this rule applies: the higher an item is in the list of priorities, the more detail is needed about it so it can be actioned as quickly as possible.

But be careful: In the early stages user stories can be nebulous at best, and that's just fine. It makes no sense - in fact, it's against the rules of Scrum - to clarify every item on the list right at the start. You have to let them grow.

Emergent means that items gradually move up the list in the product backlog. At first they are low priority, but as the project goes on become more important and more precise. This means they make their way up the backlog. Think of it like cooking ravioli. At first they sit on the bottom of the pan, but as they cook they rise to the top where you lift them out and set them to one side. As the Product Owner you are the cook, always putting new ravioli into the pan, letting them cook and then removing them. You don't want the pan empty, and you don't want too many floating up all at the same time. Any item at the top of the product backlog can be implemented in a sprint. Everything lower down still has time in terms of implementation and detail.

As you go on, you should continually **estimate** the scope of each item. What resources will it require, and are they actually available? Is it described in enough detail to be actioned? Does it have to be done now, or can it wait? Can it be implemented within budget, or will it cost more? These questions all help estimating each item as precisely as possible.

Having done this, you're ready to move to **prioritisation**. This is the most important part as it has a direct impact on the work of the development team. Only high priority items will be included in a sprint. As Product Owner it's up to you to decide what is important and what's not, and this should be recorded in the backlog.

Items and User Stories

As we saw above, the best way to describe features and requirements in Scrum is as a user story. This means describing a feature from the perspective of the person who will ultimately use it. You can use this sentence as a template:

"As (role of the user) I want to (feature, function) so that (advantage)."

You can write these stories on cards, adding further information (such as a link to a website which already has this feature) and set out the conditions that have to be met for the feature to be successful. These are also known as **Conditions of Satisfaction**. One very simple example would be a website that can be read in portrait mode, but which is also mobile friendly.

The scale of a user story depends on its purpose. At first your Stories will probably be very abstract as you try to draw out the main connections. In doing this, you are clarifying the job the software you're working on has to do. This kind of all-encompassing story is often known as an 'Epic', a bit like 'War and Peace' or 'Game of Thrones'. But these epics can quickly be broken down into smaller stories until they reach a scale the developers can actually work with. In practice it often makes sense to indicate stories that are derived from the epic, perhaps by using a key word, a certain colour or a card where all the connections are recorded. You could also see it as a kind of cover sheet.

Developing Stories

At the beginning of the Scrum project you have an idea or an order, but no user stories. So the first thing you should to is round up your stakeholders, the Product Owner, Scrum Master and your development team and start developing your stories. Don't forget, though, that this is only the first step - the stories will change over time. The first meeting is usually quite long and can last a few hours or even days, depending on the scope of the project: it's a kind of brainstorming. The structure of these meetings will be shaped by your team and how they work. Some like to break stories down while others will immediately start thinking of features. The art is in making sense of all this later. Mind maps - especially electronic ones - can really help with this. When you're brainstorming, don't worry too much about hierarchies and structures: just make sure you get all the information down. If you prefer working on paper, try setting up several boards to represent different levels with Post-It notes to add ideas to each.

As the facilitator of these meetings you need to clearly define the roles included in the user stories. A user can be:

- The end-user who installs the app on their phone
- A colleague from Marketing who needs to analyse the data
- A representative from HR who wants to ensure that the app is accessible.

Try using the old trick from advertisers who want to ensure their campaigns are personalised around specific target audiences. You try to describe your customer, even going so far as to visualise them. You can use this when drawing up your user roles - try giving them names for a bit of fun, too.

Let's assume you're developing an AR app which superimposes information onto the camera image in certain locations. You might imagine your user as a 30-year-old man who likes tech, is called Josh and has a medium to high level of income.

So the story might look like this:

Josh wants to see the offers and discounts in the stores he passes in the street so he doesn't have to go in and ask about them.

This is only a suggestion - you're free to write the stories any way you wish, just as long as they're clear and meet the DEEP rules.

Maintaining the Backlog

While development is underway the backlog should never be completely empty or fully completed. The Product Owner should always be checking, adding data, making changes and maintaining it. user stories should be refined, and reprioritised. It may be that an item which had been low priority needs to be quickly moved up the priority list, but without impacting work on other important things. The good thing about Scrum is that new ideas and experiences are always coming in, but the challenge is to handle these without bringing the backlog into confusion. A well maintained backlog is essential to the success of a project.

Who adds to the Product Backlog?

Because Scrum and teamwork go hand-in-hand, anyone involved in a project can work on the product backlog. At first this will generally be the stakeholders as they contribute their wishes. As the project moves forward, the developers will come in, submitting change proposals, recording errors or specifying where they need more information. The key thing is that developers should be working on the backlog throughout. There's no specific timescale set down in Scrum, but the Product Owner has to make sure the backlog is in constant motion. But it's also important to consult the stakeholders to check whether what's happening is in line with their ideas, or if changes are needed. If you are developing a navigation app, for example, a new map provider might enter the market offering a cheaper and better alternative. That can mean that you either have to test the maps or check whether the new maps can be integrated into your existing items and increments.

When can an item be removed?

Returning to our ravioli, you only take them out when they have floated up to the surface of the pan. In the language of Scrum, this is their 'Definition of Ready'. Each item needs its own description of what it will look like when it is complete before it can be removed. The description needs to be suffiently detailed that the developers can get to work on it right away and implement it in a sprint. The rules of Scrum require a Definition of Ready, but they don't specify what one should look like. That means you can work out with your team which criteria have to be met for the developers to start working on an item. But so you don't have to reinvent the wheel, here are some tips to help you draw up your own criteria:

clear: Everyone needs to understand the item from technical and functional perspectives.

feasible: The item can be delivered within budget and makes financial sense.

detailed: It contains all necessary technical details and dependencies on other items.

independent: It can be delivered on its own and in one go.

testable: It will be ready for testing as soon as its development is complete.

reviewable: The Scrum Team must be able to review the item in the sprint review.

But there are some critics who warn against defining these criteria too narrowly. The essence of Scrum is in change, and if you spend too much time worrying about rules then you lose sight of the big picture. By looking at the Definition of Ready the development team should be able to tell if an item is ready, but that doesn't mean that only items meeting these criteria can be removed from the backlog. What it really means is that the development team is responsible for the product backlog and should be thinking about this themselves throughout. It's up to you how important each of these criteria is, but don't forget you can all too quickly end up erecting barriers to a smooth and effective workflow.

Side-Note: Finances

The product backlog has no maximum limit. The only limit to be aware of is the project budget. It's your job as Product Owner to break the budget down and allocate it to user stories and items as necessary. You will need a precise itemisation of costs arising from the development.

Manpower costs can be controlled by the pace of the work. For example, if you want to deliver 10 **story points** per sprint, with each sprint lasting two weeks, and you've said that the project will require 160 story points, then it will take 16 sprints to reach your goal - or, put differently, 32 weeks. Then you multiply this number by your manpower costs and divide it by 52 (weeks). This gives you your estimated manpower costs for the project. After this you can add in other costs such as rent, hardware, licences etc to reach your final cost. You should never lose sight of the importance of not just staying within budget, but making a profit.

You can calculate your profit in a range of ways. The most important consideration is when you will reach the profit zone. The shorter the development time and the lower the costs, the sooner you'll move into the black. In International projects this is also known as the payback period. It can also make sense not to develop the software in the first place, and instead look to rent or buy a similar solution - this is often the case with internal projects. In doing this you can calculate which solution or timescale will be most economical. The third component is ROI. This is basically the point when the product has made enough profit to cover all the costs of developing it. Velocity also plays a role in this, but it is a business component.

Here are some of the other terms which are frequently used in connection with financial issues:

Earned Value. This refers to the value of all completed "potentially shippable products" or items which fulfil their Definition of Done.

Cost Variance is the difference between how much has been spent (Actual Costs, AC) and the EV (Earned Value).

The **Cost Performance Index (CPI)** calculates the ratio of Earned Value to Actual Costs - EV/AV. A CPI of more than 1 means that we are earning more from the project than we spent on it. If the value is less than one then there's a risk we won't cover our costs and we will go over budget.

As Product Owner you're not expected to be a management expert, but it is definitely your job to monitor costs and assess stories against their business value.

5.2.2 The Sprint Backlog

If there are enough fully developed and refined user stories in the product backlog to undertake a sprint, the they are committed to the sprint backlog. Think of it as a to-do-list for the development team. The development team breaks each item into its own sprint tasks. These are generally highly technical and minutely detailed. While you can maintain the product backlog well with cards, tables are often required for sprints. One such table might have the following headings:

- Description
- Start
- Scheduled Duration
- Owner (Developer)
- Progress
- Timetable (in weeks)

5.2.3 Sprints (Increments)

Sprints are the part of Scrum where items are taken out of the product backlog and developed. The golden rule is that they must have a fixed duration, usually two weeks in length. In a sprint two things cannot be negotiated: how long it lasts and what it will accomplish. As soon as one sprint ends, the next one automatically starts. So that this flow isn't broken, the Product Owner and development team must work together on planning sprints. The outcome of a sprint is called an increment.

Planning a Sprint

Both parties must agree on what a sprint is going to achieve. Usually this will be listed as an essential feature in the product backlog, but it will still have to be converted into a concrete sprint. When the sprint is being planned you should discuss which items will be removed from the product backlog. Generally these will the items with the highest priority, though there may be times when other linked items are included for implementation in a sprint. The sprint planning meeting is day 0 of a sprint and it's the time when everyone discusses what can be achieved by the end of the sprint. Once everyone has agreed the items to work on then developers (and usually the Scrum Master, too) sit down and decide what is needed to achieve each feature. That might look like this:

- Feature: Window overlay in camera display
- Tasks: Design - 4 hours
- Implementation in CSS - 4 hours
- Coding - 16 hours
- Testing - 4 hours

The developers will know best how to organise themselves, so it's essential that the only person working with them at this stage is the Scrum Master. If you are the Product Owner, then you play no part in this process. You have to trust your team to deliver the sprint successfully. But you also have to be on hand if they have any questions. It's up to the team to ensure that the work proceeds smoothly. You should also be thinking about what can be developed in parallel and what is which tasks depend on others. So in the example above, while the CSS developers are waiting on the designers, the coders can get on with the design.

There's no ideal number of items which can be worked on in any single sprint. It depends on the product, the size and experience of the development team and, most importantly, how well they work together. The more they help each other out, the more work can get done. Someone who only ever works on their own is not an ideal person to have in a Scrum team. The same applies to specialists who know nothing about anything outside their own area.

You need to be aware of your team's abilities before you decide how much work you can assign to them. Sprints aren't about getting as much work done as possible in a short space of time. What really matters is achieving your goal and delivering real progress on your product.

How your team organises itself and works together will decide the success of your project. Scrum is a method that is only ever as good as the people who are working in it. At the beginning of a sprint you discuss the resources needed for each task. And of course you need to make sure nothing goes to waste. A coder shouldn't be sitting around waiting for the UI, and a tester should always be ready to work on little increments, instead of waiting for the final product. At the end of the sprint you should have a shippable product - that is, something which works and has financial value.

The tasks are best displayed on a table known as the taskboard. This allows each member of the team to decide which task they are going to work on. This doesn't mean, though, that they are solely responsible for it. They can ask for help at any time: what matters is getting the work done, not who does it.

It's also important that progress is recorded. In Scrum this is done on something called a Burndown Chart. This shows actual progress along an ideal line. The Y axis shows the amount of work (in hours) remaining, while the X axis shows the time elapsed with sprints. As the project goes on the chart is added to. This allows you as Project Owner to see how close you are to achieving your goals. If the ideal line is below what has actually been done, then it means progress is too slow. You are at risk of failing to deliver a successful result. If the record of progress is below the ideal line, then the team is working faster than expected - generally a good thing, as it means they might finish sooner. But if this is the case in several successive sprints, it might also tell you that you have too much resource in the project or not enough tasks for the team to work on.

Another way to measure progress and the hours required is to calculate the velocity of a project. The velocity of a sprint is defined as:

Velocity = Developers x Hours x Working Days

The hours measure work done, not just hours in the office. You'll see that the velocity changes often. This can happen for a range of reasons: Some tasks are easier and some teams are quicker. At the beginning the velocity tends to be lower as teams get used to the task. The velocity should pick up quickly - if this doesn't happen, it's up to you to find out why. Velocity can be visualised as a graph, just like the burndown chart.

Capacity

Capacity is something that is often underestimated It's just a question of how many people are in a team, how resilient they are and how much work they can do in a given period of time. When planning a sprint it's all too easy to be over-optimistic about this. Everyone's excited about the project and say, "Yeah, we can do this." However, after a few sprints have gone by it becomes clear that the velocity is dropping further and further because there's just not enough capacity and the developers are exhausted. When you plan a sprint the thing you need to pay most attention to is realistic timescales. A sprint may last two weeks, but no-one works 24 hours a day. In reality, in a normal 5-day week that makes "only" 10x8=80 working hours. From that you need to take away the daily Scrums (10 x 15 minutes - that's 2.5 hours). And there are those activities which are part of working life but don't count towards the sprint itself, such as maintaining the backlog and working on other projects. A team member might fall ill or take a vacation: all those hours need to be deducted as well. It's best to build in a buffer of hours set aside for general activities so you get a realistic idea of how much capacity you really have.

Using a table with one column per team member can help with this: they should each enter how many days or hours they are available, how many hours they need for other projects or activities, and how many hours a day they generally work. You end up with the real number of hours for each team member.

Planning Poker

The developers of Scrum came up with a great way of bringing a bit of fun into the planning process amid what can otherwise become a procession of dull meetings: Planning Poker. The aim is to estimate the complexity and/or relative target values in product development. Numbered cards are played face down and revealed at the same time, and everyone discusses the choices.

> How to play:
>
> You need a game master - they won't be playing the game themselves. The Product Owner gives a short summary of the user story which is to be estimated. The team can then come up with questions to make sure everyone involved understands the story. Then all players select the card from their stack which represents their estimation and play it face down on the table. The number on the card can represent days or hours, but most games use story points (see below).
>
> Everyone then discusses how the players arrived at their estimation. At a predetermined time (an egg-timer can be a good way of stopping discussions going on too long) all the cards are turned over at once. The players with the highest and lowest values explain briefly why they chose this timeframe. Then the

estimators reselect a card and play it face down. The point of planning poker is not to win, but to play a game whose aim is reaching consensus. With each new round the highest and lowest values should be justified, until everyone agrees on a value. When they have done, the next user story is read out. It's essential to record the key points of the discussion and record them in the documentation for the product item.

Story Points

'Story Points' are a measure of the total effort required by a product backlog item in numerical form. What the actual number is really doesn't matter. It's about their relative values. So, for example, a story of value 4 is twice as big as a story of value 2. It's also half as big as 8 and one third the size of 12. Some teams prefer to work with big numbers. It's up to you to decide what works for you. Many Scrum teams like to use a simplified version of the Fibonacci sequence: 1, 2, 3, 5, 8, 13, 20, 40, 100.

But how do you decide how much effort is needed? This method brings together the real time in hours with the complexity of the work as well as the risks and uncertainties associated with it.

Let's imagine you're developing a website. One item is a contact form with ten fields; the other is a page which just contains one picture. The effort required for the contact form is much greater - more html will need to be written - and more complex, too, because the team will need to programme how the data is to be transferred. As well as this, you'll need to include testing the item. The form also presents a greater risk, as even a tiny error can result in your data going walkies and not coming back.

There's no magic formula which shows how you convert these three elements into story points. You will have to estimate yourself and compare the items carefully. A good way of doing this is for your team to agree on one story as the basis for their calculations. It should be easily estimated, such as inserting a picture into a website. That would be a 1 or a 2.

One common mistake is to confuse the effort represented by story points with hours. Story points don't express actual hours, just relative amounts of time. They help make estimations which are not just determined by time alone. And in the end they are an aid to the Product Owner in prioritising items in the backlog. However, they can also be used to calculate the return of investment on an item.

But story points should never stop the development team taking stories out of the product backlog. Imagine a case where you have two stories of identical priority but one has fewer story points and the other a large number. That should never lead the developers to take the smaller one just because it's simpler and quicker to implement. What matters more than any tool is developing the product as quickly and as effectively as possible.

Tracking Time in Scrum

Even if the sprints are measured in days and hours and the time required for certain user stories is taken into account in the sprint planning, the use of time recording systems among Scrum users is still controversial. Some argue that these systems are a waste of time and mean unnecessary bureaucracy. You probably experienced this yourself on traditional projects, spending all your time recording how long you had been working for (and asking yourself while you were doing it whether you should be recording that time as well).

But there are good reasons to record time, too. On the one hand it can set the basis for calculating costs to customers. Many don't just want to pay for the results, but also want to know how much effort went into achieving them. It's also important to the Product Owner to know how long the developers are taking. It's the only way they can check whether the estimates arrived at during the spring planning correspond with reality. There can also be a legal requirement to record time, such as when calculating overtime.

The point is not so much about monitoring performance but to use the past as a way of learning for the future. If you do employ a time recording system then you need to explain to your team that it's not about supervising your colleagues.

Nowadays nobody needs to write anything down by hand any more. There are software packages which recognise when someone starts work - they can be started manually or automatically and provided with data about the project. This reduces the administrative load to a minimum and still provides the Product Owner with valuable information.

However, you should not treat this data as the decisive basis for making decisions. They are just parameters which show trends - much like the burndown chart. Think of them as a refinement of the burndown chart. You should always have a discussion with your team about how time is to be recorded so that they spend as little time as possible doing it. You should also discuss the time recording in the context of your sprint retrospective: is it helpful, or is it putting a brake on your team? As long as there are no legal or contractual grounds for keeping these records, they can always be negotiated as the project goes on.

And if your customer demands to see timesheets, do everything you can to talk them out of it. In the end, Scrum is about delivering valuable work in a short time. If you're billing by the hour it will just slow the project down unnecessarily, because you, dutifully observing your financial responsibilities, will try to sell as many hours as possible.

6. The Daily Scrum

One of the most important tools for finding consensus is the daily Scrum. When the sprint is going on you want your team working, not worrying about organisational matters. But to allow a continuous flow of ideas and access regular feedback a daily Scrum takes place every 24 hours. This is a meeting for everyone on the development team which lasts exactly 15 minutes. The Scrum Master can lead it, but they don't have to. The procedure generally runs like in this way.

Every team member gives a pithy answer to the following questions:

- What have I achieved in the last 24 hours?
- What will I do in the next 24 hours?
- What impediments are there to my progress?

Everyone knows what everyone else has done, what they're doing and the difficulties they may face. These difficulties are not addressed in the daily scrum itself, but at a later time between team members themselves, or in discussion between the Scrum Master and the Product Owner, for example when it concerns technical issues such as server performance.

The aim of every daily scrum is to get all members of the team in sync. A good place for this is the kitchen area: you can't sit down there, and that helps keep everyone to the 15 minute rule.

Don't confuse the daily scrum with a detailed progress check. It is not about submitting reports and there is no expectation that participants should do so. Most importantly, the meeting is not there to try to organise progress into a plan. This is why the time allowed is so short: it is a chance to give a quick update on problems and successes.

After the meeting everyone gets back to work and carries on dealing with outstanding tasks. Not that they should all be sitting in silence and staring at their screens, though: Communication is always essential. When the daily scrum is over small groups will often meet to discuss issues arising. Sometimes a team member will need advice or help from colleagues. At the end of the day the team add the hours worked to the burndown chart.

6.1 Definition of Done (DoD)

As well as deciding the tasks to put into a sprint, you also need to define the criteria that have to be fulfilled to say that a task is finished. This usually takes the form of a checklist which sets out the criteria for a deliverable product. Exactly what goes on the checklist is decided during the sprint planning - examples from older projects can help with this - and they are compiled by the development team. Below is a list of elements commonly used on these lists to help you get started:

- X% of code complete

- Successful tests for the user story

- All acceptance criteria fulfilled

- Documentation available

- Non-functioning elements successfully tested

- Code counter-checked by another colleague

- Software running on the test server

- Technical documentation compiled

- Legal documentation (e.g. licences) compiled

- No bugs discovered

- Localisation available

- Interface open

- Hardware successfully tested

- Performance tests passed

This list is only a suggestion, and your Definition of Done will be dictated by your project and its scope. Whatever happens, there has to be a Definition of Done. They should never be touched up to allow someone to register a success. If an increment hasn't been tested, then it will behave accordingly. Later in the book you will find some tips on how to respond if this happens to you. That said, it's not the end of the world if one element in the checklist isn't ticked off.

As with everything else in Scrum, the checklist is not set in stone. As the project goes on the checklists can change, especially when it comes to testing. So it might happen that one criteria for an increment in a website is that certain features have to be running in a test environment. However, it may happen that at the end of a few sprints the results have been so successful that you can go live straight away. What this means is that future increments will need to be running on the live server.

You may remember that user stories can also be assigned conditions of satisfaction. When stories are processed in a sprint, their conditions of satisfaction have to be fulfilled, too. If you're developing a payment gateway, for example, that might mean that Visa, Mastercard, Maestro, Amex, Apple Pay and Google Pay have to work so the gateway can count as being successfully developed. As a rule, the conditions of satisfaction can be more clearly examined after the Definition of Done has been reached. The story is only accepted only when the increment is done and the item criteria are fulfilled.

After two weeks the sprint is finished and the moment of truth arrives. The team members can look at the burndown chart and see which way the trend is going. You can get much more a much more detailed analysis in the sprint review.

6.2 Documentation

One reason there is so little love for classic projects is the enormous outlay of time putting together reports. Because the emphasis in a Scrum project is shifted onto communication and teamwork, those involved do not have to justify every last thing they do. Not that this means there should be no documentation at all. Rather, documentation exists so that work can be done efficiently. It is based on the product item. The product backlog documents the procedure, the Definition of Ready, the conditions of satisfaction and, later, the Definition of Done. In the early stages the design of an item will be discussed and written down. Later the code will be added along with the UI, and, as soon as testing is possible, their design and results will be added, too. What sets Scrum apart from a traditional project is that documentation is developed 'on the job', rather than compiling a huge tome at the end of the project which no-one will ever look at again. In Scrum, by contrast, the documentation exists to serve transparency and communication. Everyone has access to it and can see what the status of an item is and what has gone into it.

There are three simple rules for great documentation:

Essential

Only document as much as you really need - no more. It must be precise enough to be understood but you don't want a whole book: it's about creating value for others. Documents are put together so they can be used again in future, not because someone said they have to be.

Timely

Documentation goes on alongside development, firstly because it saves time and secondly because it makes information available immediately. The data that goes into the document is data which contributes to understanding the product, not just offering a retrospective on the work that's already been done.

Valuable

Everything that happens in Scrum should have a value, so your documentation should be valuable, too. And that means that the value of your documentation must be greater than the cost of writing it.

Test-Driven Design

One of the key features of the Scrum framework is test-driven design where are written before any coding takes place. You will also hear people using the phrase "Test before software" to describe how the developers orientate themselves around testing. This means the programmer knows exactly what test the code has to pass when they begin writing it. These tests have a similar function to requirements, but this is where you need to exercise a degree of caution as they can imply a degree of restriction on the developer who might consider the test conditions more important than the product itself. Keep a close eye on this, ensuring that the necessary balance is maintained so that design and test conditions are treated as one and the same.

Before the programmer writes any code they draw up the test which it has to pass. Testing in the early stages will always have a low success rate, but as the development progress goes on the results will continually improve. While Scrum is generally already a test driven design due to the short sprints, this principle is also applied to how tasks are processed.

7. The Sprint Review

It is worth carrying out the review a few days before the end of the sprint itself. This leaves some time leftover to make changes and achieve the goal of a potentially shippable product. The development team, the Scrum Master, Product Owner and the stakeholders take part in the sprint review. The stakeholders are an important part of the meeting as they bring an external perspective on the product increment and can provide valuable insights. This might happen when you've been working on a payment gateway and shortly before completion you receive an e-mail from business development telling you that a contract has been signed with Apple Pay which needs to be built into the product.

There may also be times when colleagues from other divisions attend the sprint review, though they otherwise have had little to do with the project. You should always facilitate this, as long as the meetings aren't allowed to go on too long.

Just as for any meeting, preparation is key to an effective sprint review. You need to

- know who should be invited
- set a date
- check that all the sprints are complete
- prepare demonstrations
- decide who's going to lead the meeting
- decide who will present the demonstrations

Of course, it's never easy to find a time when everyone is available, but the sprint review is a key element of Scrum and should never be skipped.

Demonstrations are only presented for "done" tasks. If the sprint review is taking place before the end of the sprint, then there may be some tasks which aren't done yet. It makes sense for the Product Owner to check in with the development team to find out which tasks have been completed and can be taken to the sprint review. It's quite normal for some tasks to be incomplete, but you should be able to bring most increments to the sprint review.

The sprint review is a working meeting. It's your chance to bring everyone up to speed and get their input. It's not a shop window for the programmers and developers, and certainly not the chance for the Product Owner to show off. For that reason, there's no place in sprint reviews for PowerPoints and all the usual formalities of meetings in large organisations. The quicker the work gets done, the better. It makes most sense if the Scrum Master leads the meeting, because they are in the best place to decide what is and is not important, and to step in if needs be.

A Sprint Review Agenda

First, describe what the sprint was to **achieve** and what was being worked on. Briefly present each product item that was taken out of the backlog and put into the sprint.

Next, give an **overview** of what was achieved in the sprint. The taskboard can help here, though of course you shouldn't get bogged down in the details. There may well still be some tasks open at this stage, and it's fine to allow a constructive discussion of why this is the case. However, it's not the time to call individuals to account, but to work together to analyse the causes. Sometimes the wrong task was included in a sprint, or there was not enough resource available, or the required hours were just wrongly estimated.

Next come the **demonstrations**. This is a chance for the to present products and increments. In the world of game and website development this is generally very easy as so much is done with graphics. When working on software, though, demonstrations can be very dry - especially early on - while the code cannot yet be represented visually. How much code to present will depend on who is taking part in the meeting. The demonstrations present progress, but they are only one part of the sprint review.

Every demo should be **discussed**, along with any other done increments. This is the key focus of the meeting, and it's essential that the stakeholders get the chance to express their views. Are they happy with what has been done? Does it meet their expectations? Do they want to suggest any changes or developments? Encourage criticism, as without feedback the team cannot improve. These discussions often influence the product backlog, such as using learnings from the sprint to review priorities for future sprints. You may decide that the Definition of Ready needs to be adjusted because too many items are not yet in the position to be worked on.

Many Scrum users see the review as a final sign-off for the team, but this is a misconception. An item is finished when it meets the Definition of Done and the Product Owner has accepted it. The review is a chance to analyse products, not to release them. In practice you will often find that increments are handed back after the review for the Product Owner to reconsider their decision. If this happens, it should be the exception, not the rule, and it should not delay the flow of sprints.

8. The Sprint Retrospective

Scrum doesn't mean getting rid of all meetings - you'll need plenty of them - but they work differently to traditional projects. Alongside the sprint review, which is concerned with increments, at the end of every sprint there is also a sprint retrospective. This is focused on analysing the sprint itself. Was the right number of tasks removed from the backlog, or were there too many? What did we do well, and what didn't go so well? This is also your chance to analyse velocity. As Scrum measures sprints by the hour or days, it's important to work out how fast your team is working - this will allow you to apportion resources as effectively as possible. We discussed how velocity is calculated in an earlier chapter. Causes for a team operating too slowly can include a lack of resources, the wrong combination of people, having to work on too many items or not having enough detail about the items they are working on. The sprint retrospective is the right time to dive into these questions.

The retrospective can be led by a team member or the Scrum Master - it's often advantageous to rotate who leads the meeting. Only members of the development team take part in the meeting. Some people invite the product owner, though that can bring disadvantages as well as advantages. If you've got a strong relationship with your Product Owner, then it can make a lot of sense to have them there.

As with any part of a Scrum project, the retrospective needs to meet some basic requirements. Scrum meetings are:

- Planned around a specific time slot (timeboxed)
- Goal-orientated
- Action-orientated

This means you allot a certain amount of time for the meeting and it will apply to all retrospectives. Experience shows that between 90 and 120 minutes are a good timeframe. Within this time you will need to discuss the following points:

- Sum up where you are
- Additional information and discussion
- Decide how to solve problems
- Wrap-up

Some Scrum teams even set specific amounts of team to each of these activities. You can leave this decision to your team, but it should go on to apply to all future meetings. Often the discussions take up the lion's share of the time, and the wrap-up can be accomplished in a few meetings.

Think of the retrospective as a debriefing, much like a football team will do after a match. Even if you won, you still need to analyse the game so you can perform better in future. The difference is that there is no manager - the Scrum Master is responsible for motivating the participants, but they don't decide the formation. Deciding who takes on the role is a collaborative decision, made during the sprint planning. As a project goes on you may find that changes are needed, and these can be discussed during the retrospective.

You will often hear that you have to gee up your team members to bring ideas along to the retrospective. This assumes that the specialists are generally a quiet bunch who would prefer to get on with their individual work than to see the big picture. If your team members fit this pattern, then you picked the wrong team. A Scrum team is not just a group of nerds, but a collective of people who possess what are known as T-shaped skills. This means they combine broad knowledge (the upper part of the T) with deep specialist skills and abilities (corresponding to the vertical). It's up to the Scrum Master to develop these qualities, such as through activities like brainstorming and mind-mapping, or just collaborative games. All that matters is that the meeting delivers a result.

Product items that are not done by the end of a sprint

At the end of every sprint there will be some items which are not yet complete. They have not fulfilled their Definition of Done. This is annoying, but it's not a disaster - just don't forget to include the "but". Even if you're under tremendous time pressure, if something isn't done, you must not say it is.

You put the unfinished parts of the item back into the backlog and assign them a new priority. On the one hand this prevents the documentation going awry, and on the other, it allows you to estimate the work required in the next sprint. But there are no fixed rules here. Some Scrum users feel it is more transparent if only the remaining work goes back into the backlog as a new item, but others make the decision on a case-by-case basis. It could simply have been that the item was too big and needs to be broken down into smaller chunks, or perhaps the user story wasn't quite right. The same applies when you are estimating velocity: should you count a sprint that was broken off?

Whatever you do, don't just push the incomplete items automatically into the next sprint. Every sprint needs to be planned afresh and started with a blank sheet of paper. There may be exceptions in the case of priorities in the product backlog. You may think about whether you assigned the right number of story points. You may also need to adjust your Definition of Ready, depending on the criteria which were and were not met.

9. When Scrum projects fail

It's a fact of life that some Scrum projects cannot be brought to a successful conclusion. This can have any number of causes, but let's discuss a few of the so you can guard against suffering them in your own project.

Everyone's doing it

Everyone's talking about Scrum right now, and it's become almost an article of faith for new start-ups. You'd be hard-pressed to find an IT consultant who isn't also offering their services as a Scrum Master. But just because everyone's doing it doesn't mean that Scrum is right for your project. Even if you are a software developer there are methods - Agile or not - that can achieve success. Whatever you do, you need a framework in which you can reach your goals and is right for your situation.

The team doesn't fit

You won't always be in the position to choose your own team: in large companies especially you'll have to work with developers who are already in place, and sometimes you'll be given a Product Owner who doesn't really want to do the job. A Scrum project can only work if everyone is pulling in the same direction. Sometimes it can also be down to the personalities involved. For example, some developers prefer to work alone and aren't used to helping others. Or they may just be overwhelmed if they have only worked in other systems up till now (and perhaps quite rightly maintain that those worked very well for them). You can train and motivate your team, but sometimes it just won't be enough.

It's the wrong project

There's an old saying that goes, "To the man with a hammer, everything looks like a nail", and this can be true of Scrum as well. Some projects are too big to manage with Scrum, and others are not suitable in terms of their objectives. Scrum won't help you build a new airport, and it makes no sense to assemble a Scrum team for a straightforward website. Scrum may be too informal to deliver the level of compliance with legal requirements for sensitive or secure projects. These may demand forms of documentation which simply do not fit into a Scrum framework, causing disruption to performance and slow progress. And if a customer comes to you with a complete list of images, navigation and a selection of fonts, then a developer can get on with that without needing to start a Scrum project.

The environment is too disruptive

Scrum is about flow (something it shares with old-style waterfall projects), so even the smallest disruption can have negative consequences for success. In large organisations such disruptions are part of everyday life. Another department might poach a member of your team or say you have to assemble a new team altogether. You might get an unexpected promotion: great for you, but it means your team loses their Scrum Master or Product Owner. You may be subject to an unexpected audit, and, instead of working on sprints, your team has to answer questions from business consultants. There's nothing you can do to stop or guide such processes. All you can do is solve the problem and then check your charts to see if the project is still running as planned or if the disruption has caused delays.

10. Scrum in other industries

Agile development has its roots in lean manufacturing, which was principally developed by the car industry. It's no surprise then, that Scrum is being employed outside the software industry. Construction is another equally dependent on project management. Every building project is faced with the same challenges as developing a piece of software. There are countless little details to be realised, and every day new challenges, problems and change requests arise.

A fascinating study was carried out in Switzerland, where Scrum was used during the construction of a four-storey apartment building. The development team was made up of three architects, a construction engineer, an engineer, an accountant and an interior designer. It was managed somewhat unusually in that the architects and the Scrum Master themselves maintained the product backlog, owing to time issues affecting the owner. Initially each sprint lasted five days, but this soon proved to be insufficient and they were extended to two weeks. The team worked with taskboards and Trello, an app that helps teams spread across different physical locations. What was missing from this project, though, was the builders themselves. If the foreman had been included, then the focus would have been more on the actual construction than just the planning.

Scrum has even been employed in hospitals, where there are some striking similarities to observe. Each patient is their own little Scrum project. The morning rounds are akin to the Daily Scrum, whereby everyone involved in the patient's care can be brought up-to-date on their condition. Even before the patient is admitted the participants had made a diagnosis and drawn up a treatment plan. Hospital treatments rarely last long, as the aim is to free the bed up again as quickly as possible. This means that the treatment should be constantly adapted. Each round of treatment equalled one task. The individual needs of each patient dictate how long a sprint should last: two weeks or less. The Definition of Done could be the patient's discharge from hospital, a return to normal blood levels or a broken bone being found to have healed.

Wholesalers also use Scrum. They are often faced with the challenge of synchronising hundreds of suppliers with their own systems. This can lead to problems if you have several branches and warehouses. Scrum can help if you take each warehouse as its own scrum project. The goal is to provide the suppliers with the best possible conditions. Each supplier is an item in the product backlog (defined, for example, by their requirements and delivery terms), and the Definition of Done is a checklist which the supplier has to tick off so that deliveries can be carried out smoothly (such as night deliveries, container size and so on).

Here are some tips which can help you deploy Scrum in creative environments such as marketing, or even in your law firm.

1. Write down the jobs that have to be done (this is your backlog).

2. Define each item concisely (this is the user story). Postcards work great for this: you just pin them up on a notice board.

3. Call your team together and talk them through the cards on the wall.

4. Then discuss what your priorities are.

5. Set the timeframe for the work (the sprint). Two or three weeks are a good starting-point.

6. Share out the cards with your team according to their priority. You might find a Kanban board very helpful with projects like this. These consist of four columns: To Do, In Progress, On Hold and Done.

7. Move the cards across the columns depending on their status. The On-Hold column does to an extent contradict the principle that an unfinished item should not be returned to the product backlog, but in smaller project it can be useful.

8. Whatever happens, make sure you meet every day. A quarter of an hour is enough to bring everyone up-to-date and address problems.

9. Once you've completed a cycle, meet with your team to discuss the problems that arose and how you can avoid them in future.

10. You should also meet with your stakeholders after each cycle to determine if the current status of the project is in line with their expectations and whether to proceed at this pace.

11. Software for Scrum

There would be a certain irony to using Scrum to develop software without using software to support your work. In truth, it is entirely possible to run a project without technological support - all you need is some paper and a flipchart. But you'll see very quickly that a dedicated package can make life much easier.

There's a huge market for Agile software, ranging from all-inclusive packages to simple time recording and to-do-lists.

One of the leading providers is **Axosoft**, who offer a SaaS package as an in-house solution. It helps you compile and handle your product backlog, and it also offers a Daily Scrum tool. It's a fantastic tool for the Scrum Master just as much as the Product Owner. The collaborative interface makes it possible for your team to get as much information as possible and store it as documentation. It's used by firms such as Boeing and Cisco.

VersionOne was developed for Agile projects and can also be used in Scrum projects. It's like a cockpit for the Scrum Master and Product Owner where they can identify progress and administer tasks. Its strengths are its internal communication tools which are not unlike social media. Nonetheless, it's not a pure Scrum application, so you may find you never actually use a lot of its features.

Yodiz was developed in Finland as a dedicated Scrum tool and it has rapidly gained a large following. It's one of the best tools for planning sprints, maintaining the backlog and it's even able to cope with epics. What's more, it comes with a bug tracking included.

If you search online for Scrum software you'll find a huge number of hits. But be warned: most of these are just project management tools that can, after a fashion, turn their hand to Agile and Scrum projects. The danger is that you'll find yourself drawn back into the old ways of project management, and that is something you'll want to avoid. Still, you have to hand it to waterfall projects that they are at least trying to build in some elements of Agile.

12. Certified Scrum Masters and Product Owners

Because getting the process right the first time you use Scrum is so important, many firms look for a certified Scrum Master or Product Owner to support the project. There are countless companies which will offer to train you up into a certified Scrum leader, offline as well as online. The question is, what do these certificates actually mean? The Scrum Alliance, for example, trains *certified* Scrum Masters and Product Owners while you become a *professional* Scrum Master with Scrum.org. These two organisations have even gone so far as to copywrite their respective terms. The good news is that there isn't really much difference between them. Most seminars offer training to help you pass the Scrum.org exam. They generally last one or two days. Often you'll be working on real examples, so that you become familiar with working with Scrum from the outset.

If you want to become a Professional Scrum Master there are three levels of certification available to you: PSM I, PSM II and PSM III. The PSM I course shows that you can demonstrate a fundamental level of Scrum mastery, understand the terminology and know how to use Scrum. The PSM II certificate demonstrates a deeper understanding of Scrum and its underlying principles, and how Scrum can be implemented in complex situations. PSM III is the boss level Scrum. It shows you can implement Scrum in any organisation, work with complex projects and understand all aspects of Scrum and Scrum values.

For the Product Owner there are two levels of Professional Scrum Product Owner: I and II. In the first course you learn about how Scrum works and the value it can bring to your products. You also learn about continued professional development. This certificate is the minimum demonstration of knowledge any Professional Scrum Product Owner should be able to make. The level II certificate demonstrates a comprehensive knowledge of Scrum, an understanding of the product backlog and the ability to lead Scrum projects with a high degree of professionalism. Holding a Level II certificate proves you are the complete Scrum professional.

That said, it is not compulsory for you attend these seminars or hold a certificate to work on a Scrum project. Nonetheless, they can be very helpful, and firms are always looking for evidence that a potential Scrum leader knows their stuff. This book will help you prepare for one of the Scrum.org tests. Whether you choose to attend an online course, a physical workshop or just rely on your experience to help you pass the test is up to you.

14. Conclusion

"Good is the enemy of great, but great
is the enemy of shipped."

Jeffrey Zeldman

We hope that this book has helped you understand the basic principles of Scrum. It can help you prepare for the Scrum Master and Product Owner tests, but it was not written only with this in mind. The aim was to give you an overview of how this form of software and product development works. And of course, practice is much more important than theory. With every Scrum project you undertake you will learn more about how Scrum works, and improve your skills as a Scrum Master, Product Owner or team member. Every project has its own challenges. Scrum will help you to master these challenges so that you have a system to hand which allows you to give your full attention to developing amazing products.

Have fun!
Markus Heimrath

Copyright and legal notice

This work including all its contents is protected by copyright. Reproduction, in whole or in part, as well as storage, processing, duplication and distribution by means of electronic systems, in whole or in part, is forbidden without the written permission of the Author. All translation Rights reserved.

The contents of this book were searched on the basis of recognized sources and examined with utmost care. However, the Author assumes no guarantee regarding the timeliness, accuracy and completeness of the information provided.

Liability claims against the author relating to the damages of any health, material or ideal nature caused by the use or non-use of the information provided for or by the use of incorrect and incomplete information are in principle excluded, so far, removed from the Author. Intentionally or grossly negligent. This book does not replace medical or professional advice and care.

This book refers to third-party content. The author expressly declares that at the time of creation of the link, no illegal content was identifiable on the pages to be linked. The Author has no influence on the related content. Therefore, the Author hereby explicitly distances himself from the content of all linked pages that have been modified after the link was set. For illegal, incorrect or incomplete content and in particular for damages resulting from the use or non-use of this information, the provider of the page in question, but not the Author of this book, is responsible.

www.ingramcontent.com/pod-product-compliance
Lightning Source LLC
LaVergne TN
LVHW010653200726
843507LV00011B/1847